2024 Financial Mastery

Beyond Saving and Spending

Matthew H. Larsen

Copyright

All rights reserved. No part of this publication may be reproduced, distributed, or transmitted in any form or any means, including photocopying, recording or other electronic or mechanical methods, without the prior written permission of the publisher, except in the case of brief quotations embodied in critical reviews and certain other non-commercial uses permitted by copyright law.

Copyright © (Matthew H. Larsen), (2024).

About the Author

Matt H. Larsen is a famous author, teacher, and financial expert who is known for coming up with new ways to handle personal finances and wealth. After working in the financial planning and investment strategy field for more than twenty years, Matthew has become a top expert in the field.

Matthew started his work in the high-stakes world of corporate finance, where he learned how to analyze investments and make long-term plans for money. He has an MBA in finance from the Wharton School and a Bachelor's degree in economics. As a result of his desire to give people the tools they needed to become financially independent, he became a personal finance consultant.

There have been times when Matthew has been a featured financial expert on TV, podcasts, and major financial publications. He is known for being able to take complicated business ideas and explain them in a way that is easy to understand and interesting. His ideas on market trends, financial strategies, and building wealth are sought after by both new and experienced investors.

Matthew is an author who has written a number of best-selling books on personal finance. All of these books are meant to help readers understand how the economy works and make smart financial decisions. His work is a mix of useful tips, examples from real life, and a deep understanding of how people think about money management.

Along with his career success, Matthew is a dedicated philanthropist who works hard to help underprivileged communities learn about money. He believes that financial education is key to reducing economic disparity and allowing individuals to build a more secure future.

Matthew's unique blend of expertise, real-world experience, and a down-to-earth approach has made him a trusted voice in the world of business. His latest book, "2024 Financial Mastery: Beyond Saving and Spending," is a testament to his dedication

to helping others achieve financial success
and security.

Table of Content

Introduction

Rethinking Financial Goals for 2024

In the rapidly changing world of finance, the year 2024 marks a pivotal moment for reevaluating and redefining our approach to personal financial management. The traditional advice of 'spend less' and 'save more,' while foundational, no longer fully handles the complexities of the modern economic climate. In this crucial chapter, we dig into the nuances of the new financial landscape and explore why traditional financial advice may fall short in meeting the needs of today's savvy investors and savers.

Understanding the New Financial Landscape

The business world of 2024 is markedly different from what it was just a decade ago. Technological advancements, the rise of digital currencies, changes in the global economy, and the shifting nature of work and income sources have all added to a new financial paradigm. This section will explore these changes in detail, discussing how globalization, technology, and changing market dynamics have reshaped the way we think about money, investments, and financial security.

Key points include:

- The Impact of Technology on Personal Finance
- Global Economic Shifts and Their Effect on Investments
- The Rise of Alternative Currencies and Digital Assets
- Changing Employment Patterns and Income Sources

Why Traditional Advice Falls Short

While the age-old advice of spending less and saving more is sound, it fails to cover the breadth of strategies needed in the modern financial era. This part of the introduction tries to dissect why traditional financial wisdom may not be sufficient in

today's context and what new considerations
need to be made.

Highlights of this area include:

- Limitations of Traditional Saving Methods in a Low-Interest Environment
- The Inadequacy of Conventional Investment Advice in a Volatile Market
- The Need for Adaptive Financial Strategies in a Changing World
- Rethinking Risk Management in Personal Finance

Chapter 1

Setting Your Ultimate Financial Resolution

In the journey towards financial mastery in 2024, the initial step is not just about setting goals, but about crafting a vision that fits with your personal values, ambitions, and real-life circumstances. This chapter leads you through the process of formulating an ultimate financial resolution that is both inspiring and practical, tailored specifically to your unique situation.

Defining Your Financial Vision

Your financial vision is more than just a set of goals; it's a comprehensive picture of what you want your life to look like, influenced by your financial choices. This section helps you build that vision, considering not just the numbers, but what those numbers mean for your life.

Key focuses include:

- Envisioning Your Ideal Financial Future: Dream big and think about what financial success truly means to you.

- Aligning Financial Goals with Life Goals: Understand how your financial choices can help you achieve your broader life aspirations.

- The Role of Values in Financial Planning: Recognize how your personal values should lead your financial strategies.

Tailoring Goals to Your Personal Circumstances

Once you have a clear vision, the next step is to tailor your financial goals to fit your unique personal and economic circumstances. This part of the chapter is dedicated to creating your financial plan.

Highlights include:

- Assessing Your Current Financial Situation: Take an honest look at where you stand financially, including income, debts, assets, and spending.

- Setting Realistic and Achievable Goals: Learn how to set financial goals that are difficult yet achievable, given your current situation and future prospects.

- Adapting Goals to Life Stages: Understand how your financial goals will easily evolve as you move through different stages of life, from early career to retirement.

- Customizing Strategies for Diverse Income Levels: Whether you're a high earner, middle-income, or on a limited budget, discover how to make the most of your financial position.

Chapter 2

Building a Strong Financial Foundation

Before you can effectively navigate the road to financial mastery, it's critical to understand and strengthen your current financial position. This chapter is dedicated to helping you assess and improve your financial health, providing a stable base from which to pursue your broader financial goals.

Assessing Your Current Financial Health

A thorough assessment of your financial health is a crucial step in building a strong base. This section guides you through a comprehensive evaluation of your current financial state, helping you understand where you stand and what areas need attention.

Key components include:

1. Net Worth Calculation: Begin by calculating your net worth — the sum of all your assets minus your bills. This gives you a snapshot of your financial situation and helps track progress over time.

2. Income Analysis: Understand the stability and sources of your cash. Are you depending on a single source or diversifying your income streams? How does your pay compare to your expenses?

3. Expense Review: Take a deep dive into your buying habits. Categorize your

expenses to find necessary costs versus discretionary spending, and look for areas where you might cut back.

4. Debt Assessment: Evaluate your debts, knowing the difference between constructive debts (like a mortgage) and destructive debts (like high-interest credit cards). Develop a plan for debt reduction, prioritize high-interest or problematic debts.

5. Emergency Fund Status: Check if you have an appropriate emergency fund to cover unexpected expenses or financial downturns. Typically, this should be enough to cover 3-6 months of living costs.

6. Insurance Review: Ensure you have appropriate insurance coverage to protect

against significant financial risks, including health, property, and possibly life insurance.

7. Investment and Savings Check: Look at your present investments and savings. Are they aligned with your risk tolerance and cash goals? Are you making the most of tax-advantaged accounts and other saving opportunities?

By thoroughly assessing each of these areas, you'll gain a clear understanding of your financial health and be better equipped to make informed decisions going forward. This foundational knowledge is important for building and keeping financial stability as you work towards achieving your ultimate financial resolution in 2024.

Creating a Robust Budgeting Strategy

A robust budgeting approach is the cornerstone of sound financial management. This section of Chapter 2 is dedicated to helping you build a budget that not only manages your current financial needs but also aligns with your long-term financial vision.

Here are the key steps and factors in crafting your budgeting strategy:

1. Understanding Your Cash Flow: Begin by getting a clear picture of your monthly income and spending. This includes not just your normal salary, but any extra sources of income, as well as all fixed and variable expenses.

2. Setting Budgeting Goals: Based on your financial estimate and vision, set specific, measurable goals for your budget. These could include saving a certain portion of your income, reducing debt, or allocating funds for investments.

3. Categorizing Expenses: Divide your expenses into groups such as necessities (rent, utilities, groceries), savings, debt repayment, and discretionary spending. This will help you see where your money is going and find areas for potential savings.

4. Prioritizing Spending: Emphasize spending on basics and financial goals. Non-essential or luxury expenditures should

be carefully managed to ensure they don't impede your financial goals.

5. Implementing the 50/30/20 Rule: A popular planning method is the 50/30/20 rule, where 50% of your income goes to needs, 30% to wants, and 20% to savings and debt repayment. Adjust these percentages to fit your personal financial situation and goals.

6. Utilizing Budgeting Tools: Consider using budgeting tools or apps to track your spending and stay on course. These tools can provide real-time insights into your financial habits and help you make changes as needed.

7. Review and Adjust Regularly: Your budget should be a living record. Regularly

review and adjust it to represent changes in your income, expenses, or financial goals. This could be monthly, quarterly, or annually, based on your needs.

8. Planning for the Unexpected: Set aside a portion of your budget for unexpected costs. This goes hand in hand with keeping a healthy emergency fund.

Chapter 3

Smart Investing for Future Wealth

This chapter dives into the heart of building future wealth through smart investing. In today's dynamic financial environment, understanding and adopting modern investment strategies is crucial for long-term financial success. This section serves as an introduction to various modern investment strategies, equipping you with the knowledge to make informed choices that align with your financial goals.

Introduction to Modern Investment Strategies

In this age of rapid technological advancements and global market connectivity, investment possibilities have significantly evolved. Here, we explore a range of modern investment strategies that go beyond standard stocks and bonds, offering a more diversified approach to growing your wealth.

1. Diversification in Investment Portfolios: Learn the importance of diversifying your investment portfolio across different asset classes (stocks, bonds, real estate, commodities) and regions to reduce risk and increase potential returns.

2. Exchange-Traded Funds (ETFs) and Mutual Funds: Understand how ETFs and mutual funds can provide a diversified investment portfolio with a single transaction, perfect for both novice and experienced investors.

3. Technology and Online Investment Platforms: Discover how technology has made investing more available and efficient. Learn about robo-advisors, online trading platforms, and how they can help in making informed investment choices.

4. Impact Investing and ESG: Explore the world of impact investing and Environmental, Social, and Governance (ESG) criteria, which focus on investing in companies that aim to create social or

environmental effect alongside a financial return.

5. Real Estate Investment Strategies: Uncover the potential of real estate investments, including standard property ownership, real estate investment trusts (REITs), and crowdfunding platforms.

6. Alternative Investments: Dive into alternative investments like private equity, hedge funds, commodities, and cryptocurrencies. Understand their risks and benefits and how they can fit into your overall investment strategy.

7. Risk Management in Investing: Learn about controlling risk in your investment portfolio, including understanding your risk

tolerance, using stop-loss orders, and the role of safe-haven assets.

8. Tax-Efficient Investing: Get insights into strategies for minimizing taxes on investment gains, including tax-loss harvesting, utilizing tax-advantaged accounts, and understanding capital gains tax effects.

9. Keeping Up with Market Trends: Understand the importance of staying informed about market trends and economic indicators, and how to incorporate this knowledge into your business choices.

10. Long-Term vs. Short-Term Investing: Discuss the differences between long-term and short-term investment plans, including

the benefits and drawbacks of each approach.

Navigating Stock Markets, Real Estate, and Alternative Investments

This section offers a deeper dive into specific investment areas: the stock market, real estate, and the world of alternative investments. Each of these areas offers unique opportunities and challenges, and knowing how to handle them is key to building a diversified and resilient investment portfolio.

Navigating Stock Markets

1. Understanding Stock Market Fundamentals: Learn about the basics of the stock market, including how stocks are

traded, market indices, and how to understand stock market trends.

2.   Developing a Stock Investment Strategy: Explore various strategies for stock market investing, from picking individual stocks to investing in index funds or sector-specific ETFs.

3.   Risk Management in Stock trading: Understand the risks involved in stock market trading and learn techniques to mitigate these risks, such as diversification and setting stop-loss orders.

4.   Timing the Market vs. Time in the Market: Discuss the debate between trying to time the market and the benefits of long-term investing, with a focus on

historical market trends and investor behavior.

Real Estate Investment Strategies

1. Types of Real Estate Investments: An overview of different types of real estate investments, including residential properties, business real estate, and real estate investment trusts (REITs).

2. Analyzing Real Estate Markets: Learn how to assess real estate markets, including factors like location, economic trends, and property valuation methods.

3. Financing Real Estate Investments: Understand the different financing choices available for real estate investments,

including mortgages, hard money loans, and crowdfunding.

4. Managing and Scaling Real Estate Portfolios: Strategies for managing your real estate investments, working with renters, and scaling your real estate portfolio.

Alternative Investments

1. Exploring Alternative Investment Options: Introduction to various alternative investments like hedge funds, private equity, commodities, and antiques.

2. Investing in Cryptocurrencies and Digital Assets: Understand the emerging world of cryptocurrencies and digital assets,

including their risks, benefits, and how they can fit into a diversified financial portfolio.

3. Venture Capital and Startup Investments: Learn about the potential of investing in startups and venture capital, including how to judge startup potential and the risks involved.

3. Sustainable and Impact Investing: Explore how to align your investments with your values through sustainable and impact investing, focusing on social and environmental effect.

Chapter 4

Advanced Saving Techniques

In this chapter, we shift our focus to sophisticated saving strategies that transcend the standard savings account. The goal is to introduce you to a variety of innovative methods that can enhance your saving efficacy, possibly accelerating your journey towards financial goals.

Beyond the Savings Account: Innovative Saving Methods

1. High-Yield Savings Accounts:
Learn about high-yield savings accounts, which offer higher interest rates compared to regular savings accounts, and how to find the best ones.

2. Certificates of Deposit (CDs) Laddering:
Understand the concept of CD laddering, a strategy that includes staggering the maturity dates of multiple CDs to balance between higher interest rates and access to funds.

3. Automated Saving Tools:
Discover how automated saving tools and apps can help you save money without having to think about it, often adding up purchases to the nearest dollar and saving the difference.

4. Health Savings Accounts (HSAs) and Flexible Spending Accounts (FSAs):
Explore the benefits of HSAs and FSAs,

which offer tax advantages for medical costs, and how to maximize their benefits.

5. Retirement Accounts Beyond 401(k)s and IRAs:

Delve into other retirement savings choices such as SEP IRAs, Solo 401(k)s, and pension plans, particularly useful for self-employed individuals and small business owners.

6. Investing in Tax-Free Bonds:

Learn about tax-free bonds, such as municipal bonds, which offer tax-free interest income, making them an attractive choice for savers in higher tax brackets.

7. Utilizing Brokerage Account Cash Management Features:

Understand how to use the cash management features of your brokerage account, which can offer competitive interest rates and easy access to investment funds.

8. Savings Bonds:

Get insights into the role of savings bonds in a savings plan, including their safety and fixed interest rates.

9. Foreign Currency Accounts and Deposits:

Explore the potential of foreign currency accounts for saving, understanding the risks and opportunities offered by currency exchange rate fluctuations.

10. Peer-to-Peer (P2P) Lending Platforms:

Learn about P2P lending platforms where you can lend money to people or small businesses online, often getting higher returns compared to traditional savings options.

11. Education Savings Accounts (ESAs) and 529 Plans:

For those saving for school, explore the benefits and limitations of ESAs and 529 plans, which offer tax advantages for education-related savings.

Harnessing Technology for Automatic Savings Growth

We explore the innovative ways technology can be utilized to boost your savings easily. With the advent of fintech (financial technology), there are numerous tools and apps meant to simplify and automate the process of saving money. This part will guide you through various technological solutions that can help in growing your savings automatically.

Automated Savings Apps: Discover apps that automatically transfer a part of your income or round up your purchases to the nearest dollar, depositing the difference into a savings account. Examples include apps that connect to your bank account and use algorithms to save small amounts of money regularly without impacting your budget significantly.

Online High-Interest Savings Accounts: Learn about the benefits of online savings accounts that often offer higher interest rates compared to traditional banks. These accounts can be linked to your main account for automatic transfers.

Investment Apps with Savings Features: Some investment apps offer features that allow you to instantly invest spare change from daily purchases into a diversified portfolio, combining saving with investing.

Digital Financial Advisors and Robo-Advisors: Explore how robo-advisors can help in creating and managing an investment portfolio, including automatically rebalancing and reinvesting dividends, which can add to your savings growth.

Direct Deposit Allocation: Understand how to use direct deposit from your paycheck to automatically allocate a part of your income to different accounts, such as a separate high-yield savings account, retirement account, or an emergency fund.

Subscription Management Tools: Use technology to handle and review your subscriptions and recurring expenses. Some tools can identify and cancel unwanted subscriptions, possibly freeing up more money to save.

Budgeting and Tracking Tools: Learn about budgeting tools that track your spending and provide insights on where you can cut back, successfully increasing your ability to save.

Automated Debt Payment Plans: Consider setting up automated plans to pay down debt, which indirectly adds to your savings by reducing interest expenses over time.

Goal-Oriented Saving Platforms: Explore platforms that allow you to set specific saving goals (like a vacation, a new car, or an emergency fund) and automatically donate small amounts regularly towards these goals.

Cashback and Rewards Programs: Understand how to utilize cashback and rewards programs effectively, where the rewards from your normal spending are automatically directed into a savings account.

By harnessing these technological tools, you can simplify and boost your savings efforts. This section empowers you with information about the latest tech-driven saving methods, making it easier to consistently grow your savings without having to actively manage every aspect of the process.

Chapter 5

Income Maximization Strategies

While managing costs and saving efficiently are vital components of financial health, actively working to increase your income can accelerate your journey to financial success. This part focuses on exploring side hustles and passive income streams as effective ways to enhance your earnings.

Exploring Side Hustles

Identifying Your Skills and Interests: Begin by examining your skills, hobbies, and interests that can be monetized. This can range from freelance writing, graphic design, to tutoring or exercise coaching.

Leveraging the Gig Economy:

Understand the possibilities in the gig economy. Platforms like Uber, Airbnb, or Upwork offer flexible ways to make extra income.

E-commerce and Online Sales:

Explore how you can create income through e-commerce platforms like Etsy or eBay, whether it's by selling handmade goods, vintage items, or dropshipping.

Creating Digital Products:

Learn about creating and selling digital products such as e-books, online courses, or stock photography, which can provide ongoing income with minimal ongoing work.

Utilizing Specialized Skills:

If you have specialized skills or professional expertise, find ways to monetize these, such as consulting, coaching, or developing niche market goods or services.

Passive Income Streams

Investment Income:

Dive into how you can earn passive income through dividends from stocks, interest from bonds, or profits from other investment vehicles.

Real Estate Rental Income:

Explore the potential of earning passive income through real estate investments, whether it's standard rental properties, vacation rentals, or real estate crowdfunding platforms.

Royalties from Intellectual Property: Understand how you can earn royalties from intellectual property, such as patents, copyrights (for authors, musicians, artists), or licensing deals.

Automated Business Ventures: Learn about setting up businesses that require minimal ongoing management but can create steady income, like vending machines or automated online services.

Peer-to-Peer Lending and Crowdfunding: Explore how investing through peer-to-peer lending sites or participating in crowdfunding projects can provide a return on your investment.

By exploring these side hustles and passive income streams, you can build additional sources of income that complement your primary earnings.

Negotiating Salaries and Optimizing Career Paths

In addition to exploring side hustles and passive income streams, an equally important aspect of income maximization is optimizing your main source of income.

Negotiating Salaries

Understanding Your Worth:

Research and understand the market rate for your job and experience level. Use this knowledge to objectively evaluate your current compensation.

Preparing for Negotiation:

Gather evidence of your accomplishments, contributions, and any additional duties you've taken on. Be ready to articulate how these have positively impacted the company.

Effective Communication Techniques:

Learn how to speak successfully during salary negotiations. This means being clear, confident, and assertive, yet open to discussion.

Timing Your Request:

Understand the best timing for pay negotiations, such as during yearly reviews, after the successful completion of a major project, or when taking on new responsibilities.

Considering the Entire Compensation Package:

Look beyond just the pay. Consider negotiating for bonuses, stock options, extra vacation time, remote work opportunities, or other benefits that are valuable to you.

Optimizing Career Paths

Work Planning and Goal Setting:

Develop a clear work plan with short-term and long-term goals. Consider where you want to be in 5, 10, or 20 years, and what steps you need to take to get there.

Skills and Education Enhancement:

Identify key skills and qualifications that can boost your job prospects and income potential. This might involve further education, certifications, or learning new technologies important to your field.

Networking and Mentorship:

Utilize networking and seek mentorships to open up new possibilities and gain valuable insights into your industry. Networking can often lead to knowledge about job openings or promotions before they are publicly listed.

Strategic Job Changes:

Sometimes the best way to improve your salary is to change jobs. Learn how to spot and seize opportunities that align with your career goals and offer better compensation or advancement potential.

Work-Life Balance Considerations:

Assess opportunities not just based on salary but also on how they fit with your general work-life balance and personal well-being.

Building a Personal Brand:

Develop a personal brand that showcases your unique skills and experiences. A strong personal brand can make you more attractive to current and future employers.

By combining effective salary negotiation methods with strategic career planning, you can greatly enhance your earning potential. This section aims to equip you with the tools and information necessary to navigate and optimize your job path for maximum income growth.

Chapter 6

Debt Management and Credit Building

Managing debt successfully and building a strong credit profile are important components of financial health. This chapter focuses on strategies for reducing debt, which can liberate financial resources for saving, investing, and achieving other financial goals. This section outlines successful strategies for reducing and managing debt.

Effective Strategies for Reducing Debt

1. Understanding Your Debt:

Start by thoroughly listing all your debts, including amounts, interest rates, and due dates. This clear understanding is important for formulating a strategy to pay them off.

2. Debt Snowball Method:

This approach involves paying off debts in order of smallest to largest, regardless of interest rate. It can build a sense of accomplishment and motivate you to keep paying down debt.

3. Debt Avalanche Method:

Contrary to the snowball method, the avalanche method focuses on paying off bills with the highest interest rates first, which can save you money over time.

4. Consolidating Debt:

Explore debt consolidation choices, like personal loans or balance transfer credit cards. Consolidation can simplify payments and possibly lower interest rates.

5. Refinancing High-Interest Debt:

Look into refinancing choices for high-interest debts, such as student loans or mortgages, to take advantage of lower interest rates and reduce monthly payments.

6. Budgeting for Debt Repayment:

Adjust your budget to put more funds towards debt repayment. Prioritizing debt can help speed the payoff process.

6. Negotiating with Creditors:

Learn how to deal with creditors. You may be able to lower your interest rates, get better terms, or even settle debts for less than the full amount due.

7. Automating Payments:

Set up automated payments to ensure you constantly pay your debts on time, which can also improve your credit score.

8. Cutting Expenses and Increasing Income:

Find ways to reduce your expenses and increase your income, which can provide extra funds to pay down debt faster.

9. Avoiding New Debt:

While working to pay off current debts, it's crucial to avoid taking on new debt, which can undermine your efforts.

10. Seeking Professional Advice:

If you're dealing with debt, consider seeking advice from a credit counselor or financial advisor who can provide personalized guidance and solutions.

By adopting these strategies, you can take control of your debt, reduce financial stress, and lay a stronger foundation for your financial future.

Improving and Maintaining Your Credit Score

A good credit score is a key component of financial health, impacting your ability to borrow money, the rates you receive, and even your job chances in some cases. This part provides guidance on how to improve and keep a healthy credit score.

1. Understanding Credit Scores:

Begin by understanding what a credit score is, the factors that affect it, and why it's important. Your credit score is a measure of your trustworthiness, based on your credit history.

2. Regularly Check Credit records:

Regularly check your credit records from the three major credit bureaus (Equifax, Experian, and TransUnion) for errors or fraudulent activity. You're eligible to a free report from each bureau once a year.

3. Managing Credit Cards Wisely:

Use credit cards carefully. Avoid maxing out credit cards, and try to pay off the full amount each month, or at least keep the balance low.

4. Length of Credit History:

Maintain order credit accounts, as a longer credit history can positively impact your score. Be cautious about opening new accounts frequently.

5. Diverse Types of Credit:

A mix of different types of credit (e.g., credit cards, auto loans, student loans) can positively affect your score, as it shows you can handle various types of credit.

6. Limiting Hard Inquiries:

Be aware of hard inquiries on your credit report, which occur when you apply for new credit. Too many inquiries in a short time can negatively impact your score.

7. Addressing leftover Debts:

Work on paying down leftover debts, especially those with high interest rates. Consider tactics like debt consolidation or refinancing for more manageable payback terms.

8. Credit Building Products:

For those with limited or damaged credit, consider products meant to build or rebuild credit, such as secured credit cards or credit-builder loans.

9. Seeking Professional Advice:

If you're dealing with improving your credit score, consider consulting with a credit counselor or financial advisor.

Chapter 7

Protecting Your Wealth

Achieving financial stability and growth is important, but equally crucial is protecting the wealth you've amassed. This chapter focuses on methods for safeguarding your assets through insurance and risk management. Understanding and implementing these tactics can help secure your financial future against unforeseen events and risks.

Insurance and Risk Management

Understanding the Role of Insurance:
Grasp the fundamental idea of insurance as a tool for risk management. It's about

transferring the financial danger of life's unforeseen events to an insurance company.

Types of Insurance Policies:

Explore different types of insurance policies, including:

1. Life Insurance:

Understand the differences between term life and whole life insurance and determine which type fits your needs based on your family structure, financial responsibilities, and goals.

2. Health Insurance:

Evaluate health insurance options, including employer-provided plans, individual health insurance policies, and supplemental health insurance, to cover medical costs.

3. Disability Insurance:

Learn about short-term and long-term disability insurance, which can protect your income in case of a disability that stops you from working.

4. Property and Casualty Insurance:

Cover your physical belongings like home and car. Understand homeowner's insurance, renter's insurance, auto insurance, and policies for special valuable items.

5. Liability Insurance:

Consider personal liability insurance to protect against court claims due to accidents or injuries for which you might be held responsible.

6. Risk Assessment and Coverage Adequacy:

Conduct a thorough risk assessment to spot possible risks to your wealth and lifestyle. Ensure that your insurance policy is adequate to mitigate these risks.

7. Insurance as Part of Estate Planning:

Incorporate insurance into your estate planning, using policies like life insurance to provide for dependents, cover possible estate taxes, or create a legacy.

8. Diversifying Investments to Manage Risk:

Learn how a diversified investment portfolio can act as a risk management tool, spreading your exposure across different assets to lower the impact of market volatility.

9. Emergency Funds for Risk Mitigation:

Understand the importance of keeping an emergency fund, which can be a lifesaver in managing unforeseen costs without derailing your financial plan.

10. Legal Measures for Asset Protection:

Explore legal measures for asset protection, such as trusts and legal structures, especially if you have significant wealth or are in jobs with high liability risk.

11. Regular Review and Update of Insurance Policies:

Emphasize the importance of regularly reviewing and updating your insurance policies to ensure they stay aligned with your changing financial situation and needs.

Estate Planning and Wealth Preservation

In addition to insurance and risk management, estate planning and wealth preservation are important components of protecting your wealth. This part focuses on strategies for ensuring that your wealth is preserved, managed, and distributed according to your wishes, both during your lifetime and after.

Estate Planning

Understanding Estate Planning:

Begin with a fundamental understanding of what estate planning involves — it's not just for the rich; it's a crucial step for anyone who wants to ensure their assets are distributed as desired.

Wills and Trusts:

Learn about the value of having a will and the different types of trusts available. Wills ensure your assets are divided according to your wishes, while trusts can offer additional benefits like tax efficiency and avoiding probate.

Beneficiary listings:

Review and update beneficiary listings on accounts like life insurance, retirement plans, and bank accounts. These designations often supersede directions in wills.

Healthcare Directives and Powers of Attorney:

Establish healthcare directives and durable powers of attorney, which allow someone to make healthcare and financial choices on your behalf if you're unable to do so.

Guardianship Designations:

If you have minor children, guardianship designations are important to ensure they are cared for by the individuals you trust in the event of your incapacity or death.

Wealth Preservation

Tax Implications and Strategies:

Understand the tax implications of your estate and apply strategies to minimize estate taxes. This might include giving assets during your lifetime or setting up certain types of trusts.

Asset Protection Strategies:

Explore legal frameworks and strategies to protect your assets from lawsuits, creditors, or other risks. This might involve setting up family limited partnerships or asset protection trusts.

Philanthropic Goals and Legacy Planning:

If you have philanthropic goals, consider adding charitable giving into your estate plan. This can be achieved through direct gifts, donor-advised funds, or private charities.

Business Succession Planning:

For business owners, create a succession plan to ensure the smooth transition of your business upon your retirement, incapacity, or death.

Regular Review and Adjustments:

Estate plans and strategies for wealth preservation should be reviewed regularly and changed as needed to reflect changes in your life circumstances, tax laws, and financial situation.

Chapter 8

Having a healthy financial mindset

Though useful tips and instruments are important, how you think and feel about money also has a big impact on your financial journey. This chapter is all about developing a good attitude about money and being financially healthy in general, which are both important for long-term success.

Step by step instructions to Have a Decent Connection with Cash

1. **Grasping Your Cash Convictions:** To begin, ponder what you think and feel about cash. Find any restricting thoughts or

unfortunate behavior patterns you might have gotten over the long haul or acquired.

2. **Schooling about cash:** Put cash into your schooling about cash. Realizing things gives you influence, and realizing about cash can give you more confidence by they way you handle your cash.

3. **Putting forth Monetary Objectives**: Make sure your monetary objectives are understood and in accordance with your ethics and objectives. Putting forth clear objectives can assist you with remaining propelled and on target.

4. **Budgeting and Financial Tracking:** Implement budgeting and tracking tools to gain control over your spending and saving

habits. Awareness of your financial habits is key to making positive changes.

5. **Emergency Funds:** Prioritize building an emergency fund to provide a safety net for unexpected costs, reducing financial stress.

6. **Debt Management:** Approach debt with a strategic plan, focused on paying it down while avoiding excessive new debt.

7. **Investment and Wealth Building**: Shift your thinking from simply saving to wealth-building through investments. Grasp the force of self multiplying dividends and long haul venture.

8. **Monetary Strength:** Develop monetary versatility by getting ready for misfortunes and adjusting to changed conditions.

Monetary Health

1. Comprehensive Methodology:
Comprehend that monetary health is interconnected with absolute prosperity, including physical, profound, and emotional well-being. Look for balance in all everyday issues.

2. Stress Management:
Recognize the effect of financial stress on your health and explore stress management methods like mindfulness, meditation, or exercise.

3. Seeking Professional Guidance:

Don't hesitate to consult with financial advisors, therapists, or counselors if you're dealing with your financial mindset or experiencing emotional challenges related to money.

4. Community and Support:

Engage with a supportive community, whether through financial workshops, support groups, or online sites. Sharing experiences and thoughts can be empowering.

5. Self-Compassion:

Practice self-compassion and avoid sharp self-criticism. Financial mistakes happen to everyone; the key is to learn and grow from them.

6. **Gratitude and Abundance attitude:**
Cultivate gratitude and an abundance attitude. Focus on what you have and the opportunities that lie ahead.

By cultivating a positive financial mindset and focusing on your general financial wellness, you can build a strong foundation for sustainable financial success and a fulfilling life. This chapter offers guidance on building a healthy relationship with money and achieving a state of financial well-being.

Balancing Financial Goals with Personal Well-being

Finding the right balance between pursuing financial goals and keeping personal well-being is crucial for a fulfilling and sustainable life. This part of Chapter 8 explores strategies for achieving harmony between your financial goals and your overall well-being.

1. **Defining Your Priorities**: Start by clearly defining your personal priorities and beliefs. What means most to you in life? Understanding your core values will guide your financial choices.

2. **Setting Realistic Goals**: While financial goals are important, set realistic and achievable targets that align with your

values and lifestyle. Avoid overextending yourself for the sake of financial success.

3. **Creating a Holistic Budget:** Develop a holistic budget that considers not only cash needs but also your well-being. Allocate funds for activities and experiences that bring you joy and add to your overall happiness.

4. **Regular Check-Ins:** Periodically assess your cash goals and well-being. Are you making progress in both areas? Adjust your goals and strategies as needed to keep balance.

5. **Financial limits:** Establish clear financial limits with yourself and others. Learning to

say no to financial commitments that don't align with your priorities is important.

6. **Work-Life Balance**: Prioritize work-life balance to prevent burnout. A demanding job or excessive focus on financial goals should not come at the expense of your health and relationships.

7. **Self-Care**: Make self-care a non-negotiable part of your habit. Whether it's regular exercise, meditation, or spending time with loved ones, prioritize activities that support well-being.

8. **Emergency Preparedness**: Build an emergency fund and insurance covering to provide peace of mind. Knowing that you have a financial safety net can lower stress.

9. **Seeking Professional advice:** If you struggle to find balance, consider speaking with a financial advisor or therapist who can provide advice on aligning your financial goals with well-being.

10. **Gratitude Practice:** Practice gratitude regularly to respect the present moment and the progress you've made. A grateful mindset can improve well-being.

Balancing financial goals with personal well-being is an ongoing process that requires self-awareness and continuous changes. By integrating these strategies into your life, you can achieve financial success while keeping a fulfilling and harmonious existence.

Chapter 9

Staying Ahead: Keeping Up with Financial Trends

The world of finance is dynamic, and staying ahead of financial trends is important for making informed decisions and adapting to economic changes. This chapter focuses on two key aspects: adapting to economic changes and leveraging financial technology and tools to enhance your financial management.

Adapting to Economic Changes

1. Economic Awareness: Develop a habit of staying informed about economic trends and global events that can affect your finances.

This includes monitoring inflation rates, interest rates, and geopolitical events.

2. **Financial Resilience:** Cultivate financial resilience by keeping an emergency fund, diversifying your investments, and being prepared for economic downturns or unexpected expenses.

3. **Risk Management:** Regularly assess your risk tolerance and change your investment portfolio accordingly. Be ready to make strategy changes if market conditions warrant.

4. **Income Streams**: Explore chances to diversify your income streams. Multiple income sources can provide security in the face of economic fluctuations.

5. **Debt Management**: Keep debt under control and ensure that your debt is manageable even in difficult economic times. Avoid overleveraging.

Leveraging Financial Technology and Resources

1. **Fintech Tools:** Embrace financial technology (fintech) tools and apps that can ease financial management, such as budgeting apps, investment platforms, and digital banking services.

2. **Online Resources**: Take advantage of online resources, including financial news websites, blogs, and educational platforms

that offer views and information on financial trends and strategies.

3. **Financial Education:** Continue your financial education by enrolling in online classes, webinars, or workshops that cover topics relevant to your financial goals.

4. **Robo-Advisors**: Consider using robo-advisors for business management. These automated systems use algorithms to make investment decisions based on your risk tolerance and financial goals.

5. **Cryptocurrency and Blockchain**: Stay informed about developments in the cryptocurrency and blockchain space, as they represent emerging trends in finance that could impact your business choices.

6. **Financial Networking:** Join online financial groups and networks to exchange ideas, share experiences, and gain insights from others in the financial world.

7. **Automation**: Leverage automation for jobs like bill payments, savings transfers, and investment contributions to ensure consistency and reduce the risk of financial oversights.

8. **Cybersecurity**: Be mindful of cybersecurity best practices to protect your financial information and assets when interacting with online financial tools and resources.

By staying informed about economic changes and utilizing financial technology and resources, you can proactively adapt to financial trends and make informed choices that align with your financial goals. This chapter provides advice on how to stay ahead in the ever-evolving world of finance.

Conclusion

Your Path to Financial Mastery

Congratulations on starting on your journey to financial mastery! This concluding chapter summarizes the key takeaways from the book and provides you with an action plan for achieving your 2024 financial strategy.

Key Takeaways

Financial Awareness:

Understand the value of financial awareness and education as the foundation for financial success.

Setting Clear Goals:

Define your financial goals, both short-term and long-term, to provide direction and inspiration.

Budgeting and Saving:

Implement effective budgeting and saving strategies to build a strong financial base.

Investing Wisely:

Learn about investment techniques and the power of compound interest to grow your wealth over time.

Debt Management:

Develop methods for managing and reducing debt to free up resources for other financial goals.

Credit Management:

Understand how to improve and maintain a healthy credit score, which is important for financial flexibility.

Insurance and Risk Management:

Protect your assets through insurance and risk management techniques.

Estate Planning:

Ensure that your wealth is kept and distributed according to your wishes through proper estate planning.

Financial Wellness:

Cultivate a positive financial attitude and prioritize your overall well-being.

Adapting to Trends:

Stay informed about financial trends and leverage technology and resources to manage your finances successfully.

Action Plan: Implementing Your 2024 Financial Strategy

Review Your Goals:

Revisit your financial goals and ensure they are SMART (Specific, Measurable, Achievable, Relevant, Time-bound).

Budgeting and Saving:

Create a detailed budget that fits with your goals. Set up automatic payments to savings and investments.

Financial Strategy:

Assess your risk tolerance and financial portfolio. Make changes if needed to stay on track with your goals.

Debt Reduction:

Develop a debt reduction plan and prioritize paying down high-interest bills,

Credit Management:

Regularly check your credit records and work on improving your credit score if necessary.

Insurance and Risk Management:

Review your insurance coverage to ensure it fits with your current needs and update beneficiaries if necessary.

Estate Planning:

If you haven't already, create or update your estate plan, including wills, trusts, and healthcare directives.

Financial Wellness:

Incorporate self-care practices into your routine and seek help if you're facing financial stress.

Staying Informed:

Stay updated on economic trends and new financial technologies that can benefit your financial strategy.

Maintaining Momentum and Building Toward the Future

Maintaining momentum and building toward the future is important for your long-term financial success. Here are some key strategies to help you stay on track and continue moving toward your financial goals:

Regular Progress Reviews:

Schedule regular reviews of your financial progress. This can be monthly, quarterly, or annually, based on your goals. Evaluate how you're doing, celebrate successes, and identify areas that need improvement.

Adjust Your Goals:

Life circumstances can change, and your financial goals may need to grow accordingly. Be flexible and willing to adjust your goals to match your present priorities and aspirations.

Automate Your Finances:

Set up automated methods for savings, investments, and bill payments. Automation ensures that you consistently make progress toward your financial goals without relying on willpower alone.

Emergency Fund Maintenance:

Continue to grow and keep your emergency fund. Having a robust financial safety net provides peace of mind and protects you from unexpected costs.

Invest Wisely:

Keep an eye on your investment portfolio and make changes as needed. Consider rebalancing your investments regularly to align with your risk tolerance and goals.

Debt Reduction:

Stay committed to your debt reduction plan. As you pay off bills, reallocate those funds toward savings or investments to accelerate your financial growth.

Continuous Learning:

Stay informed about financial trends and possibilities. Attend seminars, read books, and follow financial news to expand your knowledge and make informed choices.

Tax Planning:

Explore tax-efficient methods to minimize your tax liabilities. Tax planning can greatly impact your net worth over time.

Celebrate Milestones:

Celebrate your cash milestones, both big and small. Recognizing your successes can boost motivation and reinforce positive financial habits.

Seek Professional Advice:

Consider consulting with financial advisors, estate planners, or tax professionals as your financial situation becomes more complicated. Their expertise can help you handle advanced financial strategies.

Give Back:

As your financial situation improves, consider giving back through charity donations or volunteering.

Set New Goals:

As you achieve your original financial goals, set new ones to continue challenging yourself and working toward financial growth and security.

Remember that financial mastery is a lifelong process. It's not just about reaching a goal; it's about the process of learning, adapting, and continually improving your financial well-being. Stay determined, stay focused, and keep building toward a brighter financial future.